200 New York City Facts

JAMES CHRISTOPHER

ISBN: 9798882530739

Table of Contents

Table of Contents

Media and Broadcasting (Facts 141-160) Touches on New York's significant role in the media industry, including its newspapers, TV networks, and cultural broadcasting.

Haunted Happenings (Facts 161-180): New York City, with its rich history and countless stories, is a treasure trove of spooky and haunted tales. Here are 20 spooky and/or haunted facts about New York City

NYC Secrets (Facts 181-200): We'll complete our booklet with a final set of 20 interesting facts about New York City with a diverse range of facts covering various aspects that haven't been deeply explored yet, ensuring a well-rounded and intriguing collection.

Chapter 1: Historical Milestones
(Facts 1-20)

New York was originally called New Amsterdam by the Dutch in 1624.

It was renamed New York in 1664 when the English took control.

The city served as the capital of the United States from 1785 to 1790.

The New York Stock Exchange was founded in 1792.

The Erie Canal, completed in 1825, significantly boosted New York's economy by connecting the Atlantic Ocean to the Great Lakes.

Central Park, the first landscaped public park in the U.S., opened in 1858.

The Statue of Liberty was gifted to the U.S. by France in 1886 and dedicated in New York Harbor.

Ellis Island operated as an immigration station from 1892 to 1954, processing over 12 million immigrants.

The first subway line in NYC opened in 1904.

The Harlem Renaissance in the 1920s and 1930s celebrated African-American culture.

The Empire State Building was completed in 1931 and stood as the world's tallest building for nearly 40 years.

The United Nations Headquarters was established in New York City in 1952.

The Stonewall Riots in 1969 marked the beginning of the modern gay rights movement.

The World Trade Center's Twin Towers were completed in 1973 and tragically destroyed in the terrorist attacks of September 11, 2001.

Times Square is named after The New York Times, which moved its headquarters there in 1904.

The Brooklyn Bridge, completed in 1883, was the first steel-wire suspension bridge.

New York City consists of five boroughs: Manhattan, Brooklyn, Queens, The Bronx, and Staten Island, consolidated in 1898.

The New York Public Library, one of the largest public libraries in the world, was established in 1895.

The Holland Tunnel, opened in 1927, was the first vehicular tunnel under the Hudson River.

Coney Island was one of the world's first amusement parks, opening in the 19th century. Coney Island featured various amusement parks over the years, including Steeplechase Park (opened in 1897), Luna Park (opened in 1903), and Dreamland (opened in 1904).

Chapter 2: Iconic Architecture and Landmarks (Facts 21-40)

The Chrysler Building, known for its Art Deco architecture, was completed in 1930.

Rockefeller Center, a large complex of 19 commercial buildings, was built during the Great Depression.

The High Line, an elevated park built on a former railway track, opened in 2009. Grand Central Terminal, opened in 1913, is a world-famous train station known for its grand architecture.

The Flatiron Building, completed in 1902, is known for its unique triangular shape.

One World Trade Center, also known as Freedom Tower, opened in 2014 as the main building of the rebuilt World Trade Center complex.

The Metropolitan Museum of Art, founded in 1870, is one of the world's largest and most prestigious art museums.

The Guggenheim Museum, designed by Frank Lloyd Wright and opened in 1959, is renowned for its spiral architecture. St. Patrick's Cathedral, a Neo-Gothic-style Roman Catholic cathedral, was completed in 1878.

The Woolworth Building, once the tallest building in the world, was completed in 1913.

GUGGGGENNEUUN MRT TYUTY B

Madison Square Garden, known as "The World's Most Famous Arena," has been located atop Pennsylvania Station since 1968.

The Verrazzano-Narrows Bridge, connecting Brooklyn and Staten Island, was the world's longest suspension bridge when it opened in 1964.

The New York Public Library's main branch, with its iconic lion statues Patience and Fortitude, was dedicated in 1911.

Yankee Stadium, the home ballpark for the New York Yankees, was originally opened in 1923 and rebuilt in 2009.

The Roosevelt Island Tramway, opened in 1976, offers aerial views of Manhattan, the East River, and Roosevelt Island.

The Battery Park City, planned and built during the 1970s to the 1980s, is a residential and commercial neighborhood on the west side of Lower Manhattan.

The American Museum of Natural History, established in 1869, is one of the world's largest and most famous museums.

The Queensboro Bridge, completed in 1909, is a cantilever bridge connecting Manhattan and Queens.

Radio City Music Hall, opened in 1932, is a famous entertainment venue and the headquarters for the Rockettes.

The New York Botanical Garden in the Bronx, established in 1891, spans 250 acres with over one million plants.

Chapter 3: Cultural Fabric and Communities (Facts 41-60)

Harlem, known for its African-American heritage, was the center of the Harlem Renaissance.

Chinatown in Manhattan is one of the oldest and largest Chinese neighborhoods outside Asia.

Little Italy, known for its Italian restaurants and the annual Feast of San Gennaro, has a rich history of Italian immigrants.

The annual West Indian American Day Carnival celebrates Caribbean culture and is one of the city's largest parades.

Astoria in Queens is renowned for its diverse communities, including a large Greek population.

The Lower East Side Tenement Museum preserves immigrant stories from the 19th and 20th centuries.

Brighton Beach in Brooklyn is often called "Little Odessa" due to its large Russian-speaking community.

The Jewish Museum, founded in 1904, is one of the world's largest and most important institutions devoted to Jewish culture.

Greenwich Village has been known as a bohemian cultural center and the birthplace of the LGBT rights movement.

The annual Diwali celebration in South Street Seaport marks one of the city's prominent Indian cultural events.

Fordham University, established in 1841, is the oldest Catholic and Jesuit university in the northeastern United States.

The Bronx is recognized as the birthplace of hip hop music and culture in the early 1970s.

Washington Heights is known for its significant Dominican community and cultural influence.

The Museum of Chinese in America details the Chinese American experience.

Koreatown, located on 32nd Street in Manhattan, is known for its Korean restaurants, bakeries, and karaoke bars.

The African Burial Ground National Monument, discovered in 1991, honors the African slaves buried in Lower Manhattan during the 17th and 18th centuries.

Spanish Harlem, also known as El Barrio, is known for its Puerto Rican heritage and culture.

The annual Pride March in Manhattan is one of the world's oldest and largest LGBTQ+ pride events.

The Irish Hunger Memorial in Battery Park City commemorates the Great Irish Famine and the Irish immigrant experience in America.

The National Museum of the American Indian, located in the historic Alexander Hamilton U.S. Custom House, showcases Native American history and culture.

Chapter 4: Parks and Natural Spaces
(Facts 61-80)

The Brooklyn Botanic Garden, established in 1910, features the famous Cherry Esplanade with over 200 cherry trees.

Riverside Park, designed by Frederick Law Olmsted, stretches four miles along the Hudson River.

The New York Botanical Garden in the Bronx is a major educational and research institution and a renowned plant conservation organization.

Flushing Meadows-Corona Park, site of the 1939 and 1964 World's Fairs, is Queens' largest park.

Bryant Park, located behind the New York Public Library, is known for its seasonal gardens, free activities, and open-air library.

Governors Island, a 172-acre island in New York Harbor, offers recreational spaces, cultural events, and historical landmarks.

The Hudson River Park runs along the Manhattan side of the Hudson River and is the longest waterfront park in the United States.

Prospect Park in Brooklyn contains a 60-acre lake, the only forest in Brooklyn, and the Prospect Park Zoo.

The High Line's unique design incorporates the naturalized plantings that grew on the unused tracks and views of the city and the Hudson River.

Battery Park, at the southern tip of Manhattan, serves as the departure point for ferries to the Statue of Liberty and Ellis Island.

The Jamaica Bay Wildlife Refuge in Queens is one of the most significant bird sanctuaries in the Northeastern United States and one of the best places in New York City to observe migrating species.

Central Park's Bethesda Terrace overlooks the lake and is known for its intricate carvings that represent the four seasons.

The East River Esplanade offers waterfront views and recreational activities along the eastern edge of Manhattan.

Snug Harbor Cultural Center & Botanical Garden in Staten Island features historic buildings, museums, and a Chinese scholar's garden.

Green-Wood Cemetery, founded in 1838 in Brooklyn, is one of the city's largest green spaces and a National Historic Landmark.

Pelham Bay Park in the Bronx is the city's largest park, three times the size of Central Park, featuring miles of bridle paths and hiking trails.

The Franklin D. Roosevelt Four Freedoms Park on Roosevelt Island is a memorial to President Roosevelt and his Four Freedoms speech.

City Hall Park, located in the Civic Center district of Lower Manhattan, features paths, greenery, and a collection of historic monuments.

The Socrates Sculpture Park in Queens is an outdoor museum and public park where artists can create and exhibit sculptures and multi-media installations.

The Elizabeth Street Garden in Nolita offers a green oasis with sculptures, flowers, and community events amidst the bustling city.

New York-style pizza, known for its thin crust, was popularized by Lombardi's, America's first pizzeria, opened in 1905.

The iconic New York cheesecake is known for its rich, creamy consistency, made famous by Junior's and other delis.

Bagels, introduced by Polish-Jewish immigrants, became a New York staple, with the "everything bagel" being a local invention.

The "cronut," a croissant-doughnut pastry, was invented by chef Dominique Ansel in New York City in 2013.

Katz's Delicatessen, established in 1888, is famous for its pastrami sandwiches and has become an iconic New York eatery.

The Halal Guys, starting as a food cart in Manhattan, have popularized halal street food across the globe.

Nathan's Famous Hot Dogs, originating from Coney Island since 1916, hosts an annual hot dog eating contest on July 4th.

Zabar's, a specialty food store on the Upper West Side, has been a New York institution since 1934, known for its bagels, smoked fish, and cheeses.

The Oyster Bar in Grand Central Terminal, opened in 1913, is one of the oldest seafood restaurants in New York City.

The Rainbow Room, an iconic restaurant and nightclub at the top of Rockefeller Center, offers panoramic views of Manhattan.

Smorgasburg, a weekend food market in Brooklyn, showcases a range of culinary delights from local vendors, representing the city's diverse food culture.

Russ & Daughters, serving the Lower East Side since 1914, is renowned for its smoked fish, caviar, and bagel and lox.

The Meatpacking District, once home to over 250 slaughterhouses and meatpacking plants, is now a trendy area for dining and nightlife.

Shake Shack, originating from a hot dog cart in Madison Square Park, has become a global fast-casual restaurant chain.

ITTLE ITALY
ITALIAN

Little Italy's San Gennaro festival includes a cannoli eating contest, celebrating Italian-American culture and cuisine.

Eataly, a large Italian marketplace featuring a variety of restaurants, food and beverage counters, and a cooking school, reflects New York's embrace of global cuisines.

The Chelsea Market, located in the Meatpacking District, is a food hall, shopping mall, and office building all in one, attracting foodies from around the world.

Arthur Avenue in the Bronx is known as the real Little Italy of New York, offering authentic Italian groceries, bakeries, and restaurants

THE 21 CLUB

The 21 Club, opened in 1929, is one of New York's most famous speakeasies from the Prohibition era, now a fine dining restaurant.

Levain Bakery, famous for its thick, gooey chocolate chip cookies, started on the Upper West Side and has become a must-visit for cookie lovers.

Chapter 6: Arts, Museums, and Entertainment (Facts 101-120)

The Metropolitan Museum of Art, one of the world's largest and most comprehensive art museums, was founded in 1870.

Broadway, the heart of the American theater industry, hosts dozens of spectacular productions each year.

The Museum of Modern Art (MoMA), established in 1929, is considered one of the most influential modern art museums globally.

The Guggenheim Museum, designed by Frank Lloyd Wright and opened in 1959, is famous for its unique spiral architecture and modern art collection.

Lincoln Center for the Performing Arts is a 16.3-acre complex of buildings in Manhattan that houses 11 resident arts organizations, including the Metropolitan Opera and the New York Philharmonic.

The Apollo Theater in Harlem, a significant venue for African-American performers, has launched numerous musical careers since opening in 1914.

The annual Tribeca Film Festival, founded in 2002 by Robert De Niro and others, showcases a diverse selection of film, music, and cultural events.

The Whitney Museum of American Art, focusing on 20th- and 21st-century American art, moved to its current location in the Meatpacking District in 2015.

The Public Theater, known for producing Shakespeare in the Park at the Delacorte Theater in Central Park, has been a staple of New York's theater scene since the 1950s.

Carnegie Hall, opened in 1891, is one of the most prestigious venues for classical and popular music in the world.

The Museum of the Moving Image in Queens, dedicated to the art, history, and technology of film, television, and digital media, opened in 1988.

The New York City Ballet, one of the foremost dance companies in the world, was founded in 1948 by choreographer George Balanchine and arts patron Lincoln Kirstein.

The annual New York Comic Con, a celebration of comic books, graphic novels, anime, manga, video games, toys, movies, and television, has grown to be the largest pop culture event on the East Coast.

The Jazz at Lincoln Center, led by Wynton Marsalis, is a venue dedicated to the performance, education, and promotion of jazz music.

The New York Philharmonic, founded in 1842, is one of the oldest symphony orchestras in the United States.

The Studio Museum in Harlem, founded in 1968, is dedicated to the work of artists of African descent.

The National September 11 Memorial & Museum, located at the World Trade Center site, commemorates the September 11 attacks and the 1993 World Trade Center bombing.

Radio City Music Hall, an entertainment venue located in Rockefeller Center, is known for the Rockettes, precision dance company.

The Intrepid Sea, Air & Space Museum, housed on the aircraft carrier USS Intrepid, features exhibits on American military and maritime history.

Broadway shows like "Hamilton," "The Phantom of the Opera," and "The Lion King" have become cultural phenomena, drawing audiences from around the world.

Columbia University, established in 1754, is the oldest institution of higher education in New York State.

The New York Public Library, one of the largest public libraries in the world, was founded in 1895.

New York University (NYU), founded in 1831, is one of the largest private universities in the United States.

The Bronx High School of Science, founded in 1938, is renowned for its rigorous science and mathematics programs.

The Cooper Union for the Advancement of Science and Art, established in 1859, offers full-tuition scholarships to all its students.

The City University of New York (CUNY), founded in 1961, is the largest urban university system in the United States. Cornell Tech, a technology-focused campus of Cornell University on Roosevelt Island, opened in 2017.

The Brooklyn Navy Yard, once one of America's premier naval shipbuilding facilities, has been transformed into a hub for tech and creative industries.

The Fashion Institute of Technology (FIT), founded in 1944, is a leading design, fashion, business, and technology college.

Silicon Alley, originally referring to the concentration of internet companies in Manhattan, has expanded to represent NYC's broader tech ecosystem.

The American Museum of Natural History, founded in 1869, is one of the world's preeminent scientific, educational, and cultural institutions.

The Juilliard School, established in 1905, is one of the world's leading music, dance, and drama conservatories.

Bell Labs, with a significant presence in NYC, has been a leader in technological innovation, contributing to the invention of the transistor and laser.

The Flatiron School, founded in 2012 in Manhattan, is known for its coding boot camps and emphasis on tech education.

Pratt Institute, established in 1887 in Brooklyn, is a leading college for art, design, and architecture.

The New York Academy of Sciences, founded in 1817, is one of the oldest scientific societies in the United States.

The Google New York office, located in Chelsea, is the company's largest office outside of its Mountain View headquarters.

The New York Hall of Science, originally built for the 1964 World's Fair in Queens, focuses on interactive science exhibits.

The Whitney Museum of American Art's Independent Study Program has been a significant incubator for contemporary artists since 1968.

New York City's Tech Talent Pipeline, launched in 2014, aims to support the growth of the city's technology workforce.

Chapter 8: Media and Broadcasting (Facts 141-160)

The New York Times, founded in 1851, is often referred to as the newspaper of record in the United States.

NBC's headquarters at 30 Rockefeller Plaza, known as the Comcast Building, is a landmark of media history.

The headquarters of the United Nations in Manhattan has been the site of major international broadcasting since its completion in 1952.

Madison Square Garden is not only a sports arena but also a major broadcasting venue for concerts and events.

The Wall Street Journal, headquartered in New York City, is one of the largest newspapers in the United States by circulation.

CBS Broadcasting Inc., with its headquarters in New York City, is one of the largest radio and television networks in the world.

The New Yorker, founded in 1925, is known for its rigorous fact-checking and in-depth reporting on New York City and beyond.

Bloomberg L.P., founded by Michael Bloomberg in 1981, is headquartered in New York City and is a major provider of financial news and information.

WNYC, New York's public radio station, has been on the air since 1924, making it one of the oldest public radio stations in the United States.

MTV, despite its global reach, was founded in New York City in 1981 and has influenced the music industry and popular culture.

"Saturday Night Live," broadcasting from NBC Studios since 1975, has been a staple of American comedy and a launching pad for comedians.

Times Square's New Year's Eve Ball Drop is one of the most widely broadcasted events globally, attracting millions of viewers each year.

HBO, headquartered in New York City, was the first subscription television service in the United States.

The Daily Show, a news satire and talk show, has been filmed in New York City since its inception.

The Apollo Theater's Amateur Night has been a significant venue for live performances and has been broadcasted to a wider audience.

Simon & Schuster, one of the Big Five English-language publishers, was founded in New York City in 1924.

The iconic "I Love New York" advertising campaign, launched in 1977, was a major tourism promotion effort broadcasted across various media.

Marvel Comics, headquartered in New York City, has its universe deeply rooted in the city's landscapes.

The headquarters of the Major League Baseball (MLB) Network is located in New York City, reflecting the city's importance in sports broadcasting.

Radio City Music Hall, a prominent entertainment venue, has hosted numerous televised events, including the MTV Video Music Awards.

The Dakota Building, known for its Gothic architecture, The Dakota is infamous as the site of John Lennon's murder and is said to be haunted by his ghost, among others.

The Merchant's House Museum, considered Manhattan's most haunted house, it's nearly unchanged since the 19th century and reportedly home to the Tredwell family's spirits.

The Chelsea Hotel. This historic hotel has been a creative haven for artists, writers, and musicians, some of whom, like poet Dylan Thomas and writer Thomas Wolfe, are said to still roam its halls.

The New Amsterdam Theatre. The ghost of Olive Thomas, a Ziegfeld Follies chorus girl who died under tragic circumstances, reportedly haunts the theater, especially the dressing rooms.

The Morris-Jumel Mansion, Manhattan's oldest house is said to be haunted by its former residents, including Eliza Jumel, who reportedly wanders the mansion in a purple dress.

The Conference House. Located in Staten Island, this historic house was the site of a failed peace conference during the American Revolution and is rumored to be haunted by colonial-era ghosts.

The Belasco Theatre. David Belasco, the theater's namesake and early 20th-century impresario, is said to haunt the premises, with actors reporting sightings of his ghost.

The House of Death. This Greenwich Village townhouse is reputed to be haunted by 22 ghosts, including the spirit of Mark Twain, who lived there briefly.

The Bowery Hotel. Guests and staff have reported unexplained phenomena and sightings of ghosts, believed to be remnants of the area's turbulent past.

The Ear Inn. One of the oldest bars in NYC, it's said to be haunted by a sailor named Mickey who lived upstairs in the 18th century.

The Empire State Building. There have been reports of ghost sightings on the 103rd floor, attributed to workers who died during the building's construction.

The White Horse Tavern. The ghost of poet Dylan Thomas, who drank himself to death here in 1953, is said to haunt his favorite booth.

St. Mark's Church in-the-Bowery. Peter Stuyvesant, the last Dutch Director-General of New Amsterdam, and his family are buried here, and their spirits are rumored to haunt the churchyard.

The Hangman's Elm. Located in Washington Square Park, this tree is rumored to have been used for public executions in the 18th century and is said to be haunted by the spirits of those hanged.

The Queen's House. A reportedly haunted house in Kings County, where visitors have experienced unexplained phenomena and sightings of apparitions.

GHOSTBUSTERS

The Jan Hus Presbyterian Church. This Upper East Side church is rumored to be haunted by the spirit of its namesake, Jan Hus, a Czech reformer who was burned at the stake.

The Ghostbusters Firehouse. While not actually haunted, this Tribeca firehouse became famous in the "Ghostbusters" movies and is a nod to NYC's pop culture hauntings.

The Algonquin Hotel. Guests and staff have reported sightings of the hotel's famous round table members, including Dorothy Parker, as ghosts.

The Greenwood Cemetery. One of the city's largest cemeteries, it's said to be haunted by the spirits of those interred, including famous and historical figures.

The McKittrick Hotel. While not an actual hotel, this venue for the immersive theater experience "Sleep No More" is designed to evoke a haunted hotel atmosphere, complete with eerie and supernatural elements.

New York City's haunted locations offer a chilling glimpse into the past, where history and mystery meet. Whether these stories are rooted in fact or folklore, they add a spooky layer to the city's vibrant tapestry.

Chapter 10: NY Secrets (Facts 181-200)

 Secret Tunnels Under the City. New York City is home to numerous secret tunnels and passageways, including the Atlantic Avenue Tunnel, considered the world's oldest subway tunnel.

The Hidden Beach at Fort Tilden. A lesser-known spot, Fort Tilden Beach in Queens offers a secluded and natural coastline away from the city's hustle.

The Whispering Gallery at Grand Central Terminal. This architectural feature allows whispers to be clearly heard from across the room, a result of its unique acoustical architecture.

Little Red Lighthouse. Nestled under the George Washington Bridge, this small lighthouse became famous through a children's book and is a beloved landmark.

The Elevated Acre. A hidden park located in the Financial District that offers green space and stunning views but is relatively unknown to many New Yorkers.

The Narrowest House in New York. Located at 75 1/2 Bedford Street in Greenwich Village, this house is only 9.5 feet wide but has a rich history, including former residents like Edna St. Vincent Millay.

The Berlin Wall in NYC. Five segments of the Berlin Wall are spread across the city, including locations like the United Nations headquarters and Kowsky Plaza.

The City Hall Subway Station. A beautiful, unused subway station from 1904, known for its elegant architecture, is hidden from the public eye but can be seen by staying on the 6 train after its final stop.

Rooftop Farms. New York City is home to several rooftop farms that supply fresh produce to local restaurants and markets, part of an urban agriculture movement.

The Secret Apartment at Radio City Music Hall. There's a secret apartment inside Radio City Music Hall that was designed for Samuel "Roxy" Rothafel, the theater's impresario.

The Survival of St. Mark's Bookshop. Once a cultural icon, St. Mark's Bookshop was known for its collection of literary and non-traditional works, surviving various economic challenges before finally closing.

The Poe Cottage. The last home of Edgar Allan Poe is located in the Bronx, where he spent the final years of his life and wrote some of his most famous works.

The Hess Triangle. The smallest piece of private property in the city, this tiny mosaic triangle marks a historic property dispute.

The Museum of Mathematics. An interactive museum dedicated entirely to mathematics, aiming to enhance public understanding and perception of math.

The Original Penn Station Model. A small-scale model of the original Pennsylvania Station exists, offering a glimpse into the grandeur of the lost architectural masterpiece.

The High Bridge. New York City's oldest standing bridge, which originally carried water to Manhattan as part of the Croton Aqueduct system.

The Lost Streets of New York. Hidden and demapped streets throughout the city, like the original Love Lane, offer a glimpse into the changing urban landscape

The Gold Vault of the Federal Reserve Bank. Holding approximately 6,190 tons of gold bars, it's one of the largest gold reserves in the world, located deep beneath the streets of Lower Manhattan

The Earth Room. An interior earth sculpture by Walter De Maria, consisting of 280,000 pounds of soil, located in an apartment in SoHo.

The Mysterious Bookshop. One of the oldest and largest mystery genre bookstores in the world, specializing in detective stories, thrillers, espionage novels, and more.

We hope these facts, ranging from hidden gems and architectural quirks to cultural legacies and unique installations, enrich the narrative of New York City, offering readers a deeper appreciation for its complexity and diversity.